A Great Calm

MARK 4:39 *And the wind ceased,*

and there was a great calm.

FoundationswithJanet.org

ISBN: 978-0-578-34502-4

Cover Image © Fran_kie/stock.adobe.com
Interior Book Design and Typesetting by Amanda Barnhart

© 2024 Denison Ministries All rights reserved. Scripture quotations are from The Holy Bible, English Standard Version® (ESV®) Copyright © 2001 by Crossway, a publishing ministry of Good News Publishers. All rights reserved. ESV Text Edition: 2016

JANET DENISON

A Great Calm

Finding God's Peace
when You Need it Most

with Janet Denison

Dedication

This book is dedicated to the many wonderful friends who have walked faithfully through their lives and worked to pave their journey with the strength and wisdom of Christ. Thank you for your godly witness and for teaching me the truth of Romans 8:28. You modeled the certainty that "God works all things for our good" when we live called to his good purpose.

TABLE OF CONTENTS

A note from Janet	9
Introduction	15
Tomorrow's worries are not for today	19
Wait on God by walking in his word	27
God works while we wait	35
God's timing for our journey	43
Living with consequences	51
God's occasional time-outs	59
Humility is calm confidence	67
Meekness is strength submitted	75
Pray in submission	85
Finding hope in Scripture	93
You have hope within you	103
The Good Shepherd's ministry in our lives	111
Creation reveals the greatness of God	119
The time to get ready for that day is this day	127
When the tears are ours, his peace is promised	137
You can live well, even in grief	145
Count it all joy	155
All of us need a clean heart	163
Enter faith with eyes wide open	175
Afterword: Daily pursue the great calm of Christ	183
Reflection	188

A NOTE FROM JANET

I was young and newly married when my husband and I attended a revival at our church. The preacher was a well-known pastor from a large church and his messages were excellent. On the last evening, he took questions from the congregation, and it was then that I learned an important life lesson.

Someone in the audience had just lost a spouse and wanted to know how to rebuild his life and find the strength to move on. I don't remember all the pastor said to the man that night, but he closed with a comment I will never forget.

After he had responded to the man's question, he looked at the rest of us and said, "The best time to prepare for the difficult times of life is now. Every life has times of trouble, and those times are made easier if you are already strong in the Lord."

I believed the preacher that night and, after almost forty years in the ministry, I still do.

I began writing this book as a source of help to people experiencing trials in their lives. As the writing progressed, it became a book that would also provide spiritual strength, in advance, for future trials.

The best time to prepare for the difficult times of life is now.

Everyone experiences times in their lives that are filled with anxious thoughts and difficult choices. Jesus told his disciples that this world would have troubles, but somehow the tough times still surprise us and catch us off guard.

I hope you will keep this book on a shelf or in a place where you will know you can reach for it. It will bring you comfort during those 3 a.m. moments with God. If you are headed to the hospital to see a friend, or for your own health reasons, this book would be a good companion to toss in your bag or share with your friend.

I experienced a difficult time when I often found myself up at night needing to give away the things in my life I couldn't change or fix. I realized that my need for sleep was not as important in those moments as my need for God.

God speaks to us through his word. The Bible isn't just what God said to people in ancient times; it is what God wants to say to all of us, at any time.

If we read the Bible, we can hear God speak. We can listen to Scripture like Moses listened to God, "face to face, as a man speaks to a friend" (Exodus 33:11). God speaks from the pages of your Bible. In the quiet of the night, the Lord is our voice of comfort, truth, and peace. His thoughts are what we most need to hear. His counsel will speak to the needs in our lives.

I often encourage people to turn off the news, close down the computer, dislodge the EarPods and embrace the quiet. Quiet provides a powerful peace, especially in our noise-filled culture. Psalm 23:2–3 teaches us that the Lord "leads me beside still waters. He restores my soul."

The best time to prepare for the difficult times of life is now.

But, sometimes it's the quiet we want to avoid. Why do our thoughts, our fears, and our doubts shout in the middle of the night? Almost everyone goes through periods in their life when sleep is fleeting and our thoughts are filled with ideas and worries we don't want to hear.

This book is written to help ease your mind to a biblical peace—God's great calm. We often use the Bible to strengthen our hearts and minds, but God wants to speak his peace to us from Scripture as well.

The Mayo Clinic advises, "If you wake up and can't fall back to sleep in twenty minutes or so, get out of bed. Go to another room and read or do other quiet activities until you feel sleepy." I wrote this book for your bedside table, or wherever you go when you need to quiet your mind and restore your soul. We all need moments in God's word that produce his great calm in our lives.

Most difficult times have a beginning and an end. My difficult season ended with stories of praise and answered prayers. But, even as I write those words, I know there will be more nights ahead when I will be awake, needing to pray, to seek God's peace and God's comforting calm. We aren't in heaven yet.

Our world will always be filled with noise and chaos, good times and tough times. But, God can provide the calm we need for our chaos. He wants to. That's why he made sure we could open a Bible and hear him speak. I hope this book will help God's word speak to you and provide his great calm to you any time it's needed.

We should all be able to wake up in the morning knowing it is well with my soul.

My prayer is that the Lord will use this book to do just that.

Blessings,

Janet Denison

INTRODUCTION

What is God's great calm?

Jesus had been teaching crowds of people all day on the shores of Galilee. When evening came, he told his disciples that he wanted to go to the other side of the sea. They climbed in a boat and were far away from shore when a storm blew in. Jesus was asleep in the stern of the boat and didn't wake up, even when the waves began to fill their vessel.

The disciples woke Jesus saying, "Teacher, do you not care that we are perishing?" (Mark 4:38).

There are times in our lives when we have troubled thoughts of our own.

- "Lord, are you going to do something?"
- "Do you really care?"
- "Can't you see we need help right now?"
- "But Lord, did you hear what the doctor said?"
- "Lord, will I be lonely for the *rest of my life?*"
- "Why did I say that, Lord?"
- "How could I have done that?"
- "Why didn't you remind me, God?"
- "How do I fix it, Lord?"
- "Are the best days in the rearview mirror?"

The next words of the passage reveal the heart and deity of Christ to the disciples in the boat and to all of his disciples who find themselves in their own storm today. Scripture says Jesus "rebuked the wind and said to the sea, 'Peace! Be still!' And the wind ceased, and there was a **great calm**" (Mark 4:39 emphasis added).

There was a great calm. But notice, even though the sea was calm, the disciples were not. They had just seen this man they thought of as their *rabbi* control a storm. Jesus looked at them and said, "'Why are you so afraid? Have you still no faith?' And they were filled with great fear and said to one another, 'Who then is this, that even the wind and the sea obey him?'" (Mark 4:40–41).

God's great calm is available to those who understand that Jesus is Lord of every aspect of life and, therefore, trust his perfection. But for all of us, there are times when our faith seems insufficient for our fears. We think if we could have witnessed the miracles of Christ being faithful would be easier. Remember, these same men who watched Jesus calm the storm would later run from the scene of his arrest and crucifixion. Faith can be fragile, especially in the middle of a crisis.

I once read, "Sometimes God calms the storm, but sometimes God lets the storm rage and calms his child." God's great calm is possible because he is able to speak that calm into our lives as well. Read this book prayerfully and expect God's voice to guide your thoughts. Jesus told his disciples, "The Helper, the Holy Spirit, whom the Father will send in my name, he will teach you all things and bring to your remembrance all that I have said to you" (John 14:26).

This book will help you draw near to the One who is able to rebuke the winds and calm the seas. I hope this book will increase your faith and calm your soul, even if your storms continue. May the biblical truth in these pages provide you his great calm and the strength to trust the perfection of Christ for your greatest needs.

"And which of you by being anxious can add a single hour to his span of life?"

MATTHEW 6:27

Tomorrow's worries are not for today

Jesus' Sermon on the Mount was foundational to his ministry and presented the essential principles for the Christian life. The disciples had just heard Jesus preach that sermon before they got in the boat to cross the Sea of Galilee. But had they truly heard him?

In his Sermon on the Mount, Jesus said, "Do not be anxious about tomorrow, for tomorrow will be anxious for itself" (Matthew 6:34). Jesus didn't just encourage his disciples to "not be anxious about tomorrow;" he spoke those words as a command. We can trust his words are more than just a goal or a suggestion—they are a possibility. Jesus would never give us an impossible command.

But is Christ's command doable in today's culture?

We have ten-day weather forecasts based on current satellite information. What if a hurricane or an ice storm is approaching? What if the doctor has called for a follow-up visit? What if the deal at work has fallen through? There are moments when the realities of tomorrow are all we can think about today. Is it possible not to be anxious?

The strategy for obedience is still in the command of Christ. Read his words with a first-century perspective.

The people in the first century didn't have the advance warnings we have today. Their worries were about what they couldn't know. They were the worries about the what-ifs of life.

They couldn't know if a storm was coming when they got in their boats, but they knew the winds and rains were possible. Knowing the storms might come, they got in the boat anyway.

They didn't know when an enemy was approaching, but they were aware one could. They didn't hide, consumed by worry. They lived their lives, watchfully aware.

People of the first century understood they couldn't control or deny this world's challenges.

What do you think about Jesus' command to "not be anxious about tomorrow?" Are your worries today about the what-ifs tomorrow might hold? Are you worried about controlling events that are out of your hands?

We need to adopt the first-century mindset. Jesus said tomorrow will be anxious for itself. In other words, tomorrow is just a word or an idea, not yet a reality. We are not called to be controlled or influenced by things that are only what-ifs.

We don't know what God will do tomorrow. We do know what God is doing right now. We do know what God has done. God is able to calm you in this moment. You have Jesus with you now, and you have the promise of his presence tomorrow.

Embrace the presence of Jesus right now. He is your strength for this moment. Tomorrow will take care of itself . . . tomorrow. ◆

PRAYER

Lord God, you are all I need in this moment. Fill my heart, soul, and mind with your peace, the peace that surpasses all understanding. Father, be Lord of my worries for tomorrow and the days beyond. I lay them down at your feet. Help me leave them there. I trust tomorrow will take care of itself, tomorrow. I won't worry, Lord, because you told me not to be anxious. I want to obey, so I will obey, through the power of your Holy Spirit. Amen.

A GREAT CALM

SCRIPTURE

God's word for your worries

"Do not be anxious about anything, but in everything by prayer and supplication with thanksgiving let your requests be made known to God. And the peace of God, which surpasses all understanding, will guard your hearts and your minds in Christ Jesus."

PHILIPPIANS 4:6–7

"I can do all things through him who strengthens me."

PHILIPPIANS 4:13

"And which of you by being anxious can add a single hour to his span of life?"

MATTHEW 6:27

"Therefore do not be anxious about tomorrow, for tomorrow will be anxious for itself. Sufficient for the day is its own trouble."

MATTHEW 6:34

"Fear not, for I am with you; be not dismayed, for I am your God; I will strengthen you, I will help you, I will uphold you with my righteous right hand."

ISAIAH 41:10

"Let not your hearts be troubled. Believe in God; believe also in me."
JOHN 14:1

"Therefore I tell you, do not be anxious about your life, what you will eat or what you will drink, nor about your body, what you will put on. Is not life more than food, and the body more than clothing?"
MATTHEW 6:25

"When I am afraid, I put my trust in you."
PSALM 56:3

"What then shall we say to these things? If God is for us, who can be against us?"
ROMANS 8:31

"Humble yourselves, therefore, under the mighty hand of God so that at the proper time he may exalt you, casting all your anxieties on him, because he cares for you."
1 PETER 5:6–7

"O Lord, be gracious to us; we wait for you. Be our arm every morning, our salvation in the time of trouble."

ISAIAH 33:2

Wait on God by walking in His word

Psalm 119 has 176 verses about the value of God's word to our lives. The psalm is a summary of who God is and the relationship he hopes to have with his children because they value and seek his word for their lives.

God tells us to trust his word as our guide, but that can be a hard thing to do. The Bible isn't a science book or a computer search engine. The world's answers are easily and quickly available but often based on current thinking, which often changes.

We can trust what is written in our Bibles because it has been proven truth for thousands of years. Psalm 119 describes God's word as a "lamp to our feet" pointing out our next steps. It describes Scripture as "a light to our path" showing us the way he has planned for us.

Psalm 119:105 is truth but is best understood from an ancient point of view. When the verse was written, a lamp was made to fit in the palm of the hand and *only* gave light for the next few steps. Often, God's peace arrives when we realize and accept that his word provides us needed strength and direction for our next steps, not the entire journey.

The best way to wait on God's direction for our lives is to wait in his words of direction. Study and listen to the words God will speak to you from the pages of the Bible.

We can search our computers for long-term solutions. We can hire advisors to offer their advice. But, when we pray for the needs we have right now, we are taught to trust that God will provide his answers along the way. God has taught us to remember our continuous need for him. The path is lit—for the next few steps. Take those steps and trust him to light the rest of the path as you go. His word is the "lamp to our feet and a light to our path." ◆

PRAYER

Lord, may your word give light to the decisions, the worries, and the needs I have right now. I trust you to provide your guidance for the days ahead, in the days ahead. Thank you, Lord, that for this moment you are enough. Thank you, Lord, that you always will be.

A GREAT CALM

SCRIPTURE

God's word for the wait

"I wait for the Lord, my soul waits, and in his word I hope; my soul waits for the Lord more than watchmen for the morning, more than watchmen for the morning."
PSALM 130:5–6

"The Lord is good to those who wait for him, to the soul who seeks him."
LAMENTATIONS 3:25

"Be still before the Lord and wait patiently for him; fret not yourself over the one who prospers in his way, over the man who carries out evil devices!"
PSALM 37:7

"Therefore the Lord waits to be gracious to you, and therefore exalts himself to show mercy to you. For the Lord is a God of justice; blessed are all those who wait for him."
ISAIAH 30:18

"O Lord, be gracious to us; we wait for you. Be our arm every morning, our salvation in the time of trouble."
ISAIAH 33:2

"Be patient, therefore, brothers, until the coming of the Lord. See how the farmer waits for the precious fruit of the earth, being patient about it, until it receives the early and the late rains."
JAMES 5:7

"May integrity and uprightness preserve me, for I wait for you."
PSALM 25:21

"Waiting for our blessed hope, the appearing of the glory of our great God and Savior Jesus Christ."
TITUS 2:13

"May you be strengthened with all power, according to his glorious might, for all endurance and patience with joy."
COLOSSIANS 1:11

"For through the Spirit, by faith, we ourselves eagerly wait for the hope of righteousness."
GALATIANS 5:5

"Rejoice in hope, be patient in tribulation, be constant in prayer."
ROMANS 12:12

"He who calls you is faithful; he will surely do it."

1 THESSALONIANS 5:24

God works while we wait

It would be a rare person who celebrated an opportunity to *wait*, especially if the wait is long or the outcome uncertain. It's been estimated the average person will spend six months of their lives waiting in a line. Waiting rarely seems easy or rewarding. But the Bible offers God's hope for our days of waiting.

People rarely pick up Lamentations for *good news*, but chapter 3 is rich with those verses. Lamentations 3 begins with a description of the author's many trials and hardships but concludes with all he has learned because of them. Most theologians believe the prophet Jeremiah wrote Lamentations. He lived at a particularly difficult time in biblical history. He preached to

Judah during the last forty years of its existence. He witnessed the disintegration of the nation he loved—the nation God loved. The prophet watched as the people were taken captive by Babylon. He even saw the beloved temple on Mount Zion reduced to rubble. Jeremiah knew grief and desperation at every level of life.

Yet, Jeremiah was able to praise God for his steadfast love and the fact that each morning reveals "new mercies" (Lamentations 3:22–23). Even after a long period of troubled times, the prophet is able to say to the Lord, "Great is your faithfulness" (Lamentations 3:23).

How was it possible to suffer such loss yet continue to praise?

Because the prophet had learned how to use the dark days of waiting and watching for God's good purpose. He had learned that God is good to people who wait, watching for God to work. He then teaches "it is good" for the person who waits quietly for God to save (Lamentations 3:25–26).

Waiting goes against our nature. We usually want to fix things as quickly and painlessly as possible. We know God could fix it now—if he just would. But, what if our waiting and watching for God to work is part of God's answer? If you are searching for God's "new mercies" each day, then even the tough days are an opportunity to know him more and to understand his great faithfulness to each of his children.

It is *good* to wait patiently and look for what God will do. He is merciful, he is perfect, and he is our hope. While you wait for your answers, will you watch for his? He is presently at work providing answers you didn't even know you needed. His answers to our prayers might include things we would never have asked for in the beginning.

Jeremiah had preached to the nation of Judah for years, asking them to repent and turn to God. He had called them not to settle for an appearance of faith but to genuinely worship with truth. Unfortunately, many of the people continued to go through the motions of obedient faith with unfaithful hearts. Jeremiah couldn't make the nation listen.

But some did.

Jeremiah preached to Daniel, Shadrach, Meshach, and Abednego. All of us are still learning from the prophet's words today. God didn't answer Jeremiah's prayers by saving the nation; he saved the people who turned to him. God is at work, even as we wait for *his plans*, which are our perfect answers, to unfold.

We are called to wait on God, faithfully trusting that his mercies are new each day. Great is God's faithfulness to those who are faithful to him. ◆

PRAYER

Lord, produce in me a patience born of your Spirit. I will watch for you as I wait. Help me not to miss your Presence because I'm focused on other needs. Each day brings your new mercies, and I want to receive each one. Receive my praise, as I wait, watching for you. Great is your faithfulness to me, each new day!

A GREAT CALM

SCRIPTURE

God's word for our waiting

> "Know therefore that the Lord your God is God, the faithful God who keeps covenant and steadfast love with those who love him and keep his commandments, to a thousand generations."
>
> **DEUTERONOMY 7:9**

> "God is not a man, that he should lie, or a son of man, that he should change his mind. Has he said, and will he not do it? Or has he spoken, and will he not fulfill it?"
>
> **NUMBERS 23:19**

> "If we are faithless, he remains faithful—for he cannot deny himself."
>
> **2 TIMOTHY 2:13**

> "For the word of the Lord is upright, and all his work is done in faithfulness."
>
> **PSALM 33:4**

> "The Lord passed before him and proclaimed, "The Lord, the Lord, a God merciful and gracious, slow to anger, and abounding in steadfast love and faithfulness."
>
> **EXODUS 34:6**

"Your steadfast love, O Lord, extends to the heavens, your faithfulness to the clouds."
PSALM 36:5

"He who calls you is faithful; he will surely do it."
1 THESSALONIANS 5:24

"For I know the plans I have for you, declares the Lord, plans for welfare and not for evil, to give you a future and a hope. Then you will call upon me and come and pray to me, and I will hear you. You will seek me and find me, when you seek me with all your heart."
JEREMIAH 29:11–13

"Therefore let those who suffer according to God's will entrust their souls to a faithful Creator while doing good."
1 PETER 4:19

"And we know that for those who love God all things work together for good, for those who are called according to his purpose."
ROMANS 8:28

"Jesus Christ is the same yesterday, today and forever."
HEBREWS 13:8

"I will instruct you and teach you in the way you should go; I will counsel you with my eye upon you."

PSALM 32:8

God's timing for our journey

I've often taught that one of the best indications God is at work is when the wait seems long. A lot of verses discuss this very real quality of God. He is almost always—slow. Why is that?

It seems reasonable that if God's answers were quick, his solutions might keep us from losing patience and making our own choices. We sin more often because God is slow! Why then wouldn't he *rush* to help? James, in his letter to the church, offers a good answer.

James told us that those who remain steadfast while they wait are *blessed* (James 5:11). James then reminds his readers about the steadfastness, or faithful patience, of Job. Job taught us the purpose of the Lord in working slowly to fix what is wrong. Job was *blessed and rewarded* with a steadfast faith because of the moments he waited for God to work.

God is often slow, and he does allow all of us to go through difficult, even awful times. Why? One of the most challenging aspects of our faith is that God allows his children, even his most obedient children, to suffer sometimes. If we were able, we would try to spare the people we love from suffering. But, God's ways are higher than our own. His thoughts are often not our way of thinking.

We want God to act quickly and make our troubles go away. God wants to use our troubles for his eternal purpose and our eternal reward. James reminded his readers that "the Lord is compassionate and merciful" (James 5:11). It can be very hard to believe what James wrote when we can't feel like God is being either compassionate or merciful. Our choice is to submit our feelings to what the word of God has said is true. We should trust and value God's eternal truth in Scripture more than we trust our temporal feelings.

God always cares about our earthly needs, but our eternity is his highest priority. We need to see our earthly lives as God does—simply, our journey home.

Every life journey has hills and mountains. The hard times can cause weariness and even a stumble. Sometimes we face a mountain that seems *impossible* to climb. But, God has promised to walk with us each step we take.

Endure with steadfast faith and hope, *knowing* that his eternal priorities are your blessings. Those who hike the mountains are usually stronger as a result. He wants to bless and reward this life. Even more, he wants to *bless and reward* you eternally with the treasure that lasts forever. God is slow . . . for good reasons. ◆

PRAYER

Lord, may I see you in the quiet. May I sense your work in me, even when I cannot see the work of your hands. Lord, may I wait knowing that your goals for my earthly life are often the blessings I will not receive until my life is eternal. I will walk with you, Lord, trusting your strength for the journey. I will wait for you, Lord, knowing you are slow for reasons that will matter forever. Thank you, Lord, for giving me the time I needed to be blessed.

A GREAT CALM

SCRIPTURE

God's word for your journey

"Fear not, for I am with you; be not dismayed, for I am your God; I will strengthen you, I will help you, I will uphold you with my righteous right hand."
ISAIAH 41:10

"Have I not commanded you? Be strong and courageous. Do not be frightened, and do not be dismayed, for the Lord your God is with you wherever you go."
JOSHUA 1:9

"Even though I walk through the valley of the shadow of death, I will fear no evil, for you are with me; your rod and your staff, they comfort me."
PSALM 23:4

"It is the Lord who goes before you. He will be with you; he will not leave you or forsake you. Do not fear or be dismayed."
DEUTERONOMY 31:8

"So we do not lose heart. Though our outer self is wasting away, our inner self is being renewed day by day. For the light and momentary affliction is preparing for us an eternal weight of glory beyond all comparison, as we look not to the things that are seen but to the things that are unseen. For the things that are seen are transient, but the things that are unseen are eternal."
2 CORINTHIANS 4:16–18

"I will instruct you and teach you in the way you should go; I will counsel you with my eye upon you."
PSALM 32:8

"I have set the Lord always before me; because he is at my right hand, I shall not be shaken."
PSALM 16:8

"Seek the Lord and his strength; seek his presence continually!"
1 CHRONICLES 16:11

"Count it all joy, my brothers, when you meet trials of various kinds, for you know that the testing of your faith produces steadfastness. And let steadfastness have its full effect, that you may be perfect and complete, lacking nothing."
JAMES 1:2–4

"And I am sure of this, that he who began a good work in you will bring it to completion at the day of Jesus Christ."
PHILIPPIANS 1:6

"But let justice roll down like waters, and righteousness like an ever-flowing stream."

AMOS 5:24

Living with consequences

King David understood the frustrations of living with consequences imposed by someone else. David was anointed the king of Israel long before he was given the throne. Meanwhile, King Saul was jealous and enraged and sought to take David's life. David was forced to live among his enemies, hide in caves, and wait for God's timing. Most of us will never wait for a throne like King David's, but all of us will endure the consequences that others impose on our lives.

Sometimes, through no fault of our own, we suffer. Sometimes the events in our lives are allowed by God, even when God wouldn't have chosen them for us. We live with people, and we are people, who misuse the free will given by God.

Years later, at the end of his life, David wrote a psalm about his difficult times of waiting. Psalm 37 is a chapter of wisdom written by a king who understands the pain of enduring others' ungodly choices. King David advised that we should take time to be still and wait for God to work. We shouldn't allow someone's wrong or evil choices to prompt us to make sinful choices ourselves. We should be still and wait with patience, knowing God wants to fight our battles for us. David said not to "fret over the one who prospers" or "carries out evil devices" (Psalm 37:7) and reminded us that God "loves justice" and will never "forget his saints" (Psalm 37:28).

If you are waiting for joy to return, wait knowing that God cares and will always bring his justice. You may live with the consequences of others' choices, but ultimately you will live with rewards. God blesses those times we endure, making godly choices in response.

David wrote Psalm 37 in his later years, after he had been king for a long time. By that time, he had made his own wrong choices, and others had lived with the consequences he had imposed on their lives. None of us walks through this life without causing others some harm. Paul told the church in Rome, "for all have sinned and fall short of the glory of God" (Romans 3:23). None of us will perfectly live God's plans for our lives. None of us can walk through this life without hurting another person. In fact, sometimes people are hurt *because* we walk in God's will.

King David shared encouraging words of wisdom when he wrote, "I have not seen the righteous forsaken" (Psalm 37:25).

The king gave his people this advice: turn away from what is evil, and do good instead. The rewards for that choice will be "preserved forever" (Psalm 37:28).

You can choose to do good while you wait for God to bring justice to those who do evil. We can't always avoid the consequences imposed by others' choices, but we can avoid our sinful responses. Turn away from what is evil and do good instead. Do what God is *able* to bless and he will. ◆

PRAYER

Father, it's hard to watch the wrong people win the battles. Help us know you bring justice, even when we don't see it. Lord, help us to choose a better way, a way that brings you glory. Keep us from allowing the wrong choices of others to prompt our own sins. Evil will continue to prosper on earth, but help us to choose heaven's rewards instead of earth's momentary victories. We will wait, surrounded by your presence and filled with your strength, knowing your justice is perfect—and so are your rewards.

A GREAT CALM

SCRIPTURE

God's word promises his justice

> "But let justice roll down like waters, and righteousness like an ever-flowing stream."
> **AMOS 5:24**

> "When justice is done, it is a joy to the righteous but terror to evildoers."
> **PROVERBS 21:15**

> "He has told you, O man, what is good; and what does the Lord require of you but to do justice, and to love kindness, and to walk humbly with your God?"
> **MICAH 6:8**

> "Blessed are they who observe justice, who do righteousness at all times!"
> **PSALM 106:3**

> "Therefore the Lord waits to be gracious to you, and therefore he exalts himself to show mercy to you. For the Lord is a God of justice; blessed are all those who wait for him."
> **ISAIAH 30:18**

> "Beloved, never avenge yourselves, but leave it to the wrath of God, for it is written, 'Vengeance is mine, I will repay, says the Lord.'"
> **ROMANS 12:19**

"He loves righteousness and justice; the earth is full of the steadfast love of the Lord."
PSALM 33:5

"The Rock, his work is perfect, for all his ways are justice. A God of faithfulness and without iniquity, just and upright is he."
DEUTERONOMY 32:4

"I said in my heart, God will judge the righteous and the wicked, for there is a time for every matter and for every work."
ECCLESIASTES 3:17

"Evil men do not understand justice, but those who seek the Lord understand it completely."
PROVERBS 28:5

"Judge not, and you will not be judged; condemn not, and you will not be condemned; forgive, and you will be forgiven."
LUKE 6:37

"Be still, and know that I am God. I will be exalted among the nations, I will be exalted in the earth!"

PSALM 46:10

God's occasional time-outs

We live in a culture that rewards doing more than *being*. Sometimes God calls us to simply rest, and other times God calls us to rest with a purpose. All of us who have raised kids know that sometimes we ask our children to sit down and be still. Other times, we pull a chair out and tell them to take a time-out. They *know* the difference and so should we.

If God has allowed your life to come to a standstill of some kind, ask him, "Why?" If we don't understand God's purpose for our time-out, we will likely miss his blessing.

Isaiah wrote that those who *wait* for the Lord will have their strength *renewed* (Isaiah 40:31). Isaiah said we can soar high, with wings that enable our flight with almost no effort. We simply glide with the winds provided. Just as an eagle's wings provide effortless flight, we will be able to run without growing weary. We will be able to walk through our lives without fainting and falling.

When we aren't willing to wait for the Lord to reveal his good purpose, we might find ourselves fighting the winds instead of soaring because of them. If we spend our time flapping our wings, pushing against our circumstances, we may not have the rest from our worries that God intends.

We may be anxious about many things instead of realizing we have a God who cares, as well as a God who controls. Could it be that God has blessed our busy lives with a time of waiting because he wants us to wait with him until his good purpose is revealed?

The God of all creation wants to spend time with you. He wants you to know his plans even more than you want to know them. There is *nothing* more important or more *time-sensitive* than submitting to God's time-out.

We can flap around during our time-out, or we can soar peacefully above our problems. It's not hard to know what God's purpose would be; it's just hard to choose it sometimes.

When God hands us a time-out, he has a reason. We should wait, knowing that God has blessed us and called us to a time of effortless strength. He isn't "slow to fulfill his promise" (2 Peter 3:9). God is just patient, waiting for us to catch up and catch on to the perfection of his plans. ◆

PRAYER

Forgive me, Father, for rushing ahead and resisting your plans. No wonder I am weary! Please, Father, help me wait at your feet, simply grateful for the chance to be there. I am glad for your presence, Lord. May I rest here until you lift me up. May I stay until I am ready to soar on those same winds I have fought against. In your strength, for your good purpose, I will wait for the chance to run again, and, next time, I will not grow weary.

A GREAT CALM

SCRIPTURE

God's word speaks into our times of quiet

"Come to me, all who labor and are heavy laden, and I will give you rest. Take my yoke upon you, and learn from me, for I am gentle and lowly in heart, and you will find rest for your souls. For my yoke is easy, and my burden is light."
MATTHEW 11:28–30

"Thus says the Lord: 'Stand by the roads, and look, and ask for the ancient paths, where the good way is; and walk in it, and find rest for your souls. But they said, 'We will not walk in it.'"
JEREMIAH 6:16

"Be still before the Lord and wait patiently for him; fret not yourself over the one who prospers in his way, over the man who carries out evil devices!"
PSALM 37:7

"Be still, and know that I am God. I will be exalted among the nations, I will be exalted in the earth!"
PSALM 46:10

"Therefore, while the promise of entering his rest still stands, let us fear lest any of you should seem to have failed to reach it."
HEBREWS 4:1

A GREAT CALM

"And he said to them, 'Come away by yourselves to a desolate place and rest a while.' For many were coming and going, and they had no leisure even to eat."
MARK 6:31

"So then, there remains a Sabbath rest for the people of God, for whoever has entered God's rest has also rested from his works as God did from his. Let us therefore strive to enter that rest, so that no one may fall by the same sort of disobedience."
HEBREWS 4:9–11

"The Lord is my shepherd; I shall not want. He makes me lie down in green pastures. He leads me beside still waters. He restores my soul. He leads me in paths of righteousness for his name's sake."
PSALM 23:1–3

"Your word is a lamp to my feet and a light to my path."

PSALM 119:105

Humility is calm confidence

Are you worrying about something you can't fix? We often use phrases like "It's out of my hands" or "I don't know what to do." Then, we attempt to fix what is out of our hands. Our minds can't rest until we determine what to do. Meanwhile, the apostle Peter has a surprising solution.

Much of the time our worries are rooted in our overconfidence. We worry we aren't able to do what is needed, fix what is wrong, or survive what is dangerous. We worry we aren't able when, instead, we should be confident in our *inability*.

Peter was addressing the leaders of the Christian church in Jerusalem when he said, "Clothe yourselves, all of you, with humility toward one another, for 'God opposes the proud but gives grace to the humble'" (1 Peter 5:5). When we need God's help, we could be opposing him by trying to fix it ourselves.

- Are you trying to appear confident when you are actually worried?
- Are you trying to fix what is wrong instead of recognizing you need God's answers?
- Are you asking God for solutions to a problem instead of learning *from* the problem?
- Do you want to be strong when God may have led you to a place of weakness?

Peter has an answer for our natural inclinations, which sometimes stand in opposition to God's will. Peter said, "Humble yourselves, therefore, under the mighty hand of God so that at the proper time he may exalt you, casting all your anxieties on him, because he cares for you" (1 Peter 5:6–7).

When your mind is consumed with worry, Peter's words offer a path to God's calm.

- *Humble yourself.* Recognize that our personal solutions may oppose what God wants to do in our lives and in the lives of others. We need to yield our ideas to the Lord's plans.
- *Recognize God's sovereign authority.* When we made Jesus our Savior, we gave him permission to be our Lord as well.
- *Trust God's timing.* Remember God's "proper time" is perfect and often different timing than our own.

- *Want what God wants.* Desire God's glory, God's answers, and God's solutions rather than trying to achieve something less.

Then, we can truly "cast" our worries at the foot of the throne, knowing that God loves us and will care for our worries in his perfect way. Why? Because Scripture promises that "he cares for you."

You are God's child, and you are *greatly loved* by your Father in heaven. Lay down your worries at the foot of the throne because God's solutions are perfect and ours can't be. Humble yourself so that you will *want* to submit your ideas, your solutions, and your plans to God. ◆

PRAYER

Father, I humbly submit to your perfection. I know I cannot fix what you have planned to fix yourself. I cast my worries in your direction and pray for the wisdom and strength to leave them at your feet. I am quietly confident in you, Lord. You care. You are able. You are God and I am not. I submit my choices, my will, and my answers to you. You are the Lord of my life, and I am grateful and privileged to follow where you lead.

A GREAT CALM

SCRIPTURE

God's word is God's direction

"Trust in the Lord with all your heart, and do not lean on your own understanding. In all your ways acknowledge him, and he will make straight your paths."
PROVERBS 3:5–6

"When the Spirit of truth comes, he will guide you into all the truth, for he will not speak on his own authority, but whatever he hears he will speak, and he will declare to you the things that are to come."
JOHN 16:13

"Your word is a lamp to my feet and a light to my path."
PSALM 119:105

"Make me to know your ways, O Lord; teach me your paths. Lead me in your truth and teach me, for you are the God of my salvation; for you I wait all the day long."
PSALM 25:4–5

"Seek the Lord and his strength; seek his presence continually!"
1 CHRONICLES 16:11

"And the Lord will guide you continually and satisfy your desire in scorched places and make your bones strong; and you shall be like a watered garden, like a spring of water, whose waters do not fail."
ISAIAH 58:11

"I will instruct you and teach you in the way you should go; I will counsel you with my eye upon you."
PSALM 32:8

"For all who are led by the Spirit of God are sons of God."
ROMANS 8:14

"I bless the Lord who gives me counsel; in the night also my heart instructs me. I have set the Lord always before me; because he is at my right hand, I shall not be shaken."
PSALM 16:7–8

"But seek first the kingdom of God and his righteousness, and all these things will be added to you."

MATTHEW 6:33

Meekness is strength submitted

Sometimes people question what we believe about God and the truth found in Scripture. Debates can become disagreements, and our beliefs can be treated as opinions rather than God's truth. We are told to be bold in our faith, but, at the same time, we are taught to *turn the other cheek*.

Sometimes we watch people we love choose a path we know is against God's will, even when that road may lead to short-term success or happiness. Sometimes we are the only person in the room who can't encourage their choices.

Things happen in this life that we must respond to, and other times it is best to stay silent. How do we know what to do and say? Can we know when, or if, we should respond?

Thoughts like those can shake our calm and disturb our sense of peace. We want to do the right thing, but it feels like a guess. What is the best way to determine the Lord's direction? The answer seems counterintuitive. The perfect solution isn't found in what we need to do. The perfect solution is whatever Jesus wants to do, through us.

In his Sermon on the Mount, Jesus said, "Blessed are the meek, for they will inherit the earth" (Matthew 5:5). It seems like the meek of our culture today are often the most misunderstood and underappreciated on earth. It's easy to misunderstand the words of Christ if we don't know what Jesus meant by the word *meek*.

When Jesus used the word *meek*, he used an ancient picture word describing the strength of a horse controlled by the bit in his mouth. The reason the "meek" are "blessed" is that they know how to yield or submit to the one who holds the reins.

Submission isn't a choice to be weak. Godly submission is the choice to place your strength in God's hands, yielding to God's will and ready to obey—for his good purpose.

The best way to know what to say is to know what Jesus would say and how he would say it. Sometimes the most important thing to notice is when and why Jesus would speak. Sometimes he taught his truth with directness, usually to the people who should have known better. Sometimes Jesus taught using stories, or parables, allowing people to think about what was right.

Other times, he allowed his silence to speak volumes.

When Jesus stood before the Jewish authorities on the day of his death, he stood mostly in silence. He knew those men knew what was right in God's eyes. Their blatant, self-absorbed sin was their choice, and Jesus allowed his silence to speak loudly to their hearts and minds. The story of their sin still speaks to those who will hear it. They knew what it meant to follow God and yet chose not to. They taught people every day *about* God yet didn't recognize him when he stood in their midst. That's why the Apostle Paul wrote, "All of us have sinned and fall short of the glory of God" (Romans 3:23). We have all spoken and acted like Pharisees at some point in our Christian lives.

When words are being used as weapons, sometimes silence is our most powerful message. If the people in the room know what we believe, we often don't need to repeat the biblical truth or debate it. Instead, understand that Jesus, the One who has promised to be Lord, holds the reins. Never run into a conversation if Jesus has pulled you back.

Ask him to speak through you or ask him to rein you in so your silence can speak. Either way, submit to the prompting of his Holy Spirit, seeking his perfect thoughts, words, and actions. Often, kindness, forgiveness, and grace, *delivered in meekness*, are the most important expressions in the room.

Are you worried about what to say or do? Are you frustrated and sad by the unbelief or sinful choices of those you care about? Seek the blessings that result from meekness. Take what you know and submit it to the One who knows what to say and when to say it. Blessed are the meek. They inherit the best things, the highest rewards, from their earthly lives. ◆

PRAYER

Lord, forgive us the times we have wanted to be right instead of wanting to do what you say is right in that moment. We could have been meek and submitted our words to your will. Forgive us the times we spoke truth but didn't speak it with your love and purpose in mind. Help us, Lord, to run to you before we speak. We yield our strength, our ideas, and our words to your Holy Spirit. Please, Lord, control all that we are, all that we know, and all that we are humanly capable of accomplishing. Take the reins, Lord. We want to be meek. We want to be blessed. We want to be yours.

A GREAT CALM

SCRIPTURE

God's word for the whats and whens of life

"And your ears shall hear a word behind you, saying, 'This is the way, walk in it,' when you turn to the right or when you turn to the left."

ISAIAH 30:21

"But the anointing that you received from him abides in you, and you have no need that anyone should teach you. But as his anointing teaches you about everything, and is true, and is no lie—just as it has taught you, abide in him."

1 JOHN 2:27

"For we do not have a high priest who is unable to sympathize with our weaknesses, but one who in every respect has been tempted as we are, yet without sin."

HEBREWS 4:15

"O Timothy, guard the deposit entrusted to you. Avoid the irreverent babble and contradictions of what is falsely called 'knowledge,' for by professing it some have swerved from the faith. Grace be with you."

1 TIMOTHY 6:20–21

"So we have come to know and to believe the love that God has for us. God is love, and whoever abides in love abides in God, and God abides in him."

1 JOHN 4:16

"When the Spirit of truth comes, he will guide you into all the truth, for he will not speak on his own authority, but whatever he hears he will speak, and he will declare to you the things that are to come."
JOHN 16:13

"We are from God. Whoever knows God listens to us; whoever is not from God does not listen to us. By this we know the Spirit of truth and the spirit of error."
1 JOHN 4:6

"For God gave us a spirit not of fear but of power and love and self-control."
2 TIMOTHY 1:7

"But the Helper, the Holy Spirit, whom the Father will send in my name, he will teach you all things and bring to your remembrance all that I have said to you."
JOHN 14:26

"But seek first the kingdom of God and his righteousness, and all these things will be added to you."
MATTHEW 6:33

"And we know that for those who love God all things work together for good, for those who are called according to his purpose."

ROMANS 8:28

Pray in submission

We know that God is perfect and therefore his will is perfect as well. Jesus taught us to pray, "Thy will be done." But there are times in everyone's life when our hearts can't agree with our theology. We know the words to pray, but God knows our hearts are truly praying, "*Not your will, but mine.*"

I had never struggled to pray until those times in the small hours of the morning when I had to give my child into God's hands. My oldest son, Ryan, had cancer, and we didn't know how things would turn out. He endured daily radiation treatments, and we didn't know how those would impact his future. He was a great human being, just beginning his married life, and lying on a table each day, waiting to receive the burns. My only honest prayers were, "Stop this, Lord. We need a miracle, Lord." My heart prayed, "No, Lord, not your will. Hear mine!"

I couldn't understand. I couldn't accept. I couldn't ask for anything besides what *I* wanted for Ryan's life. I struggled to care about the smaller problems other people were facing, knowing I was supposed to "love them as I loved myself"—as I loved my son. I was scheduled to get up and speak in front of a room about God's love, but I felt disappointed in what the Lord had allowed to happen. I was scared he would allow the worst. I didn't think I could love and serve God like I wanted to. Yet, somehow I did.

Actually, God loved me and I knew it. God provided his comfort when I could only grieve. God provided his love when I needed love to give. God spoke through me when I had nothing good to say myself. God provided grace for my anger, my fears, and my struggles. He told me to trust him *anyway*. All of that happened because I *prayed*.

I didn't pray "bless this food" kind of prayers. I didn't pray "now I lay me down to sleep" prayers. I prayed angry, grieving, gut-wrenching, exhausted, desperate prayers for my child. It was just God and me, in the middle of the night. Over and over, I asked, knowing it was God's choice, not mine. Over and over, I begged, knowing that sometimes cancer isn't cured.

Over and over, I prayed, knowing I was asking, "Not your will but mine," until after all my begging, I could love God—no matter how he chose to answer. What I wanted never changed, but what I was able to accept did. I prayed until I could honestly sob out the words, "Not my will, but thine."

Prayers of submission are hard. Jesus understands. Hebrews 5:7 says, "In the days of his flesh, Jesus offered up prayers and supplications, with loud cries and tears, to him who was able to save him from death, and he was heard because of his reverence."

Jesus understands how difficult it is to pray with submission. Just picture our suffering Savior in the Garden of Gethsemane, *begging* God to take the cup from him. Jesus prayed—*sweating* drops of blood— until he could say, "Not my will, but thine." Jesus was able to submit because he knew his heavenly Father, and he knew his earthly purpose.

When it seems impossible to submit to God's will, pray until you can. Those prayers won't be easy, and they usually won't be answered in the moment. But, when you revere the Creator God—truly and completely love and honor him—you can come to trust him. Only then is his will acceptable, *no matter what.*

Ryan is well, and our family has learned that we can face our greatest fears with God's strength. Our most difficult time produced God's eternal blessings. That said, every difficult time will require us to walk the uphill path through prayer until we can honestly trust that God's will is more perfect than our own. ◆

PRAYER

Father, you know what we want. Help us to know what you want. And forgive us for the time it will take us to get there. We love you, Lord. Help us to love you most. And hold us up, strengthened by your mighty hand, in the meantime. You can save, eternally. Help that to be most important even now. Give us your grace, God, until each of us is able to pray, "Not my will, not my will, not my will oh God—but thine."

A GREAT CALM

SCRIPTURE

God's word for praying for God's will

"Do not be conformed to this world, but be transformed by the renewal of your mind, that by testing you may discern what is the will of God, what is good and acceptable and perfect."
ROMANS 12:2

"I can do nothing on my own. As I hear, I judge, and my judgment is just, because I seek not my own will but the will of him who sent me."
JOHN 5:30

"Therefore do not be foolish, but understand what the will of the Lord is."
EPHESIANS 5:17

"And we know that for those who love God all things work together for good, for those who are called according to his purpose."
ROMANS 8:28

"Many are the plans in the mind of a man, but it is the purpose of the Lord that will stand."
PROVERBS 19:21

"Oh give thanks to the Lord, for he is good; for his steadfast love endures forever!"
PSALM 118:1

"Do not be anxious about anything, but in everything by prayer and supplication with thanksgiving let your requests be made known to God. And the peace of God, which surpasses all understanding will guard your hearts and minds in Christ Jesus."
PHILIPPIANS 4:6-7

"And this is the confidence that we have toward him, that if we ask anything according to his will he hears us."
1 JOHN 5:14

"Seek the Lord and his strength; seek his presence continually!"
1 CHRONICLES 16:11

"You ask and do not receive, because you ask wrongly, to spend it on your passions."
JAMES 4:3

> "Continue steadfastly in prayer, being watchful in it with thanksgiving."
> **COLOSSIANS 4:2**

> "Praying at all times in the Spirit, with all prayer and supplication. To that end keep alert with all perseverance, making supplication for all the saints."
> **EPHESIANS 6:18**

> "If any of you lacks wisdom, let him ask God, who gives generously to all without reproach, and it will be given him."
> **JAMES 1:5**

> "Pray without ceasing. Give thanks in all circumstances, for this is the will of God in Christ Jesus for you."
> **1 THESSALONIANS 5:16–18**

> "Rejoice in hope, be patient in tribulation, be constant in prayer."
> **ROMANS 12:12**

"Sanctify them in the truth; your word is truth."

JOHN 17:17

Finding hope in Scripture

We often use the various search engines on our computers to search for help with almost any questions we have. But our Bibles and Christian websites that use and teach Scripture are the best sources of hope. We need to approach the word of God with great confidence, knowing the answers we are searching for can be found.

Paul was writing to the church in Rome when he taught them to be confident in God's holy Scripture. He wrote, "For whatever was written in former days was written for our instruction, that through endurance and through the encouragement of the Scriptures we might have hope" (Romans 15:4).

Hope is a powerful, spiritual tool in our lives. With the Lord, there is *always* hope. God made certain that we would never have to abandon hope. We are promised there is no such thing as a *hopeless* Christian. He gave us the Bible, the inspired truth, so we can study, know, and base our hopes upon his words to each of us.

To understand what Paul meant, we need to define *hope* as Paul intended.

We hope people will accept our offer on a house. We hope it will be a healthy baby girl or boy. We hope they offer us the job. We hope we get an invitation. We hope it won't rain.

The kind of hope Paul was describing was different. The apostle meant: *I hope the bridge will hold. I hope the doctor will have good news. I hope the money won't run out. I hope my child will come to faith. I hope my spouse will stay. I hope there really is a heaven.*

When Paul wrote about hope, he was writing about the most important things we trust our lives to. Consider the way the word *hope* is used in the hymn:

"My hope is built on nothing less / than Jesus' blood and righteousness."

The Bible is a book of hope, showing us where to find our confidence and place our trust. But the Bible is a book to be studied. So many times I have been shown a verse, usually from a psalm, and the person asks, "Why isn't this true in my life? What did I do wrong or misunderstand?"

Sometimes we place our hope in our own understanding of a verse or passage rather than what the passage actually meant. For example, a psalm is a song of praise for what God is able to do. A psalm is not a *promise* of what God has said will always be true. It's so important to read the words and study them in the right context. It's so important to allow Scripture to mean today what it meant when it was written.

We need to place our hope in the entire truth of God's word. Our Bibles were written for "our instruction." God knew we would need hope to *endure* and to be *encouraged*. Jesus *promised*, "In the world you will have tribulation. But take heart; I have overcome the world" (John 16:33).

Our hope, biblically, isn't that nothing bad will ever happen. Scripture tells us we *will* have tough times. What is our hope? Jesus has given us the ability to overcome. We will reach the other side of a decision. We will reach the other side of our pain. We will reach the other side of an illness. We will reach the other side of this life. We can place our confident trust in the fact that no matter what this life brings, we will ultimately overcome and live with victory.

"When all around my soul gives way / He then is all my hope and stay."

Christ is our solid ground. We can stand in our salvation with confidence and great hope. Why? *Because Jesus loves us, and this we know, for the Bible tells us so.* Those simple words hold profound truth.

When you need hope, fill your life with God's perfect, holy truth—his word. He provided the inspiration and the dedication necessary so that each of us could own our Bibles, his word. May we study the Scriptures with him and for the sake of his good purpose in our lives. ◆

PRAYER

Lord, may the Bible speak to my heart and mind. May I hear your voice, your heart, and discern your will. Thank you, Father, for preserving truth and providing all we need to know you and receive your Son, our Savior. May your words provide hope for this day and hope eternal. As the hymn teaches, "All other ground is sinking sand."

A GREAT CALM

SCRIPTURE

God's word contains our hope

"For the word of God is living and active, sharper than any two-edged sword, piercing to the division of soul and spirit, of joints and of marrow, and discerning the thoughts and intentions of the heart."
HEBREWS 4:12

"Sanctify them in the truth; your word is truth."
JOHN 17:17

"Every word of God proves true; he is a shield to those who take refuge in him."
PROVERBS 30:5

"But the helper, the Holy Spirit, whom the Father will send in my name, he will teach you all things and bring to your remembrance all that I have said to you."
JOHN 14:26

"Heaven and earth will pass away, but my words will not pass away."
MATTHEW 24:35

"This Book of the Law shall not depart from your mouth, but you shall meditate on it day and night, so that you may be careful to do according to all that is written in it. For then you will make your way prosperous, and then you will have good success."
JOSHUA 1:8

"Blessed is the man who walks not in the counsel of the wicked, nor stands in the way of sinners, nor sits in the seat of scoffers; but his delight is in the law of the Lord, and on his law he meditates day and night."
PSALM 1:1-2

"His divine power has granted to us all things that pertain to life and godliness, through the knowledge of him who called us to his own glory and excellence."
2 PETER 1:3

"Do your best to present yourself to God as one approved, a worker who has no need to be ashamed, rightly handling the word of truth."
2 TIMOTHY 2:15

"Let the word of Christ dwell in you richly, teaching and admonishing one another in all wisdom, singing psalms and hymns and spiritual songs, with thankfulness in your hearts to God."
COLOSSIANS 3:16

"The grass withers, the flower fades, but the word of our God will stand forever."
ISAIAH 40:8

"Your word is a lamp to my feet and a light to my path."
PSALM 119:105

"Now faith is the assurance of things hoped for, the conviction of things not seen."

HEBREWS 11:1

You have hope within you

I have a wooden cutout I keep high on a shelf in my home. It simply reads "Hope." A friend gave it to me during a challenging time in our ministry. I remember a late-night prayer time with the Lord when I told him, "I just need some hope." But, I really didn't *need hope*; I needed to be reminded I always have hope, in Christ.

I wish I had found Romans 5:5 during those tough times! It says, "And hope does not put us to shame, because God's love has been poured into our hearts through the Holy Spirit who has been given to us." A Christian doesn't need hope; we just need to access the hope that has been poured into us.

When have you lost hope? When has this world, or someone in this world, left you feeling without hope? Quite often these days we are losing hope in our American culture, which seems to be increasingly negative about Jesus—and those who believe in Jesus. Should we still *hope* things are going to change? Should we hope for another spiritual awakening in our nation and around the world?

The answer: Of course we should hope for those things because we hope with the certainty that "with God all things are possible" (Matthew 19:26). Our hope isn't in the power of individuals to change; it is in the power of God to change individuals. And that power is "poured into" the hearts of believers through the Holy Spirit.

When the news reflects a world out of control, remind yourself Who is forever on the throne and Who controls all things.

When your witness is seen as old-fashioned, intolerant, or unrealistic, remember the reality of God's presence that the Spirit has poured into your heart.

When it feels like hope has run dry, realize that the Holy Spirit can be quenched but never removed from the life of a believer.

Jesus is with you always. He promised. There is never a moment when you do not dwell with the power of hope through the love that has been "poured into" your heart and life. Never be ashamed of your faith, of your hope, or of your godly choices.

You have a higher authority than the opinions of the world. Your standard for what is right is higher than what the world is willing to accept. You are a child of the heavenly King so of course you are different! You can hope for things the world does not expect. You can *hope all is well* when the news reports *all is chaos*.

Our hope is grounded in all that Jesus is able to do, rather than what people are capable of. We know that "with God, nothing is impossible." Our hope is poured into our hearts by the Holy Spirit himself and is limitless because he is. ◆

PRAYER

Father, when we feel hopeless, help us remember that we have been hope-filled with God's love through his Holy Spirit. We don't think like this world, hope like this world, or trust like this world. You were in the world but never of it. Help us to walk our lives with your perfect example. We always have hope because we always have you. Thank you, Lord, for loving us, filling us, and empowering us to live with your love—our hope.

A GREAT CALM

SCRIPTURE

God's word for our hope within

"Now faith is the assurance of things hoped for, the conviction of things not seen."
HEBREWS 11:1

"May the God of hope fill you with all joy and peace in believing, so that by the power of the Holy Spirit you may abound in hope."
ROMANS 15:13

"And now, O Lord, for what do I wait? My hope is in you."
PSALM 39:7

"Through him we have also obtained access by faith into this grace in which we stand, and we rejoice in the hope of the glory of God."
ROMANS 5:26

"And we desire each one of you to show the same earnestness to have the full assurance of hope until the end."
HEBREWS 6:11

"Waiting for our blessed hope, the appearing of the glory of our great God and Savior Jesus Christ."
TITUS 2:13

"Blessed be the God and Father of our Lord Jesus Christ! According to his great mercy, he has caused us to be born again to a living hope through the resurrection of Jesus Christ from the dead."
1 PETER 1:3

"So we do not lose heart. Though the outer self is wasting away, our inner self is being renewed day by day. For this light momentary affliction is preparing for us an eternal weight of glory beyond all comparison, as we look not to the things that are seen but to the things that are unseen. For the things that are seen are transient, but the things that are unseen are eternal."
2 CORINTHIANS 4:16-18

"Now may our Lord Jesus Christ himself, and God our Father, who loved us and gave us eternal comfort and good hope through grace, comfort your hearts and establish them in every good work and word."
2 THESSALONIANS 2:16-17

"I am the good shepherd. The good shepherd lays down his life for the sheep"

JOHN 10:11

The Good Shepherd's ministry in our lives

The twenty-third Psalm has often been used to bring people comfort during a time of grief, but to limit the words only to the difficult times of our lives is to miss some of its message. King David wrote the psalm as words of praise for the unending presence and purpose of God for *every* moment of life. David had been a shepherd and understood the job involved guiding and caring for his sheep. Success for a good shepherd was a flock that thrived, grew, and multiplied.

Psalm 23 teaches us how our Good Shepherd, God himself, cares for us in troubled times, but it also reveals his goal to heal and restore our earthly lives for his eternal purpose.

The key to the entire psalm is found in verse 1. David wrote, "The Lord is *my* shepherd; I shall not want." This psalm requires a spiritual commitment for each of us to consider. It doesn't say, "The Lord is *a* shepherd" or "The Lord is *the* shepherd." David used the word *my*. God honors our free will and *invites* us to be part of his flock. The comfort and message of this psalm are available to people who recognize and admit they are sheep in need of their shepherd.

God wants to give our lives his personal care and his perfect guidance, but we have to submit our own *wants* to our Shepherd's plan. So, for a time, God makes us "lie down in green pastures." He leads us "beside still waters" (V. 2).

Why are there times in our lives when we seemingly can't accomplish what we want to do? When it seems like life won't ever be the same or as good as we thought it would be? When we question God and say, "Is this all there is?" The darkest days can cause us to question how a God who loves us can allow us to suffer.

All of us go through times when life doesn't feel like it is *enough* and other seasons that feel like more than we are able to handle. We all go through times when life brings us moments we would never want or choose. King David understood those times because he lived them too. But, even earthly kings have to acknowledge they are simply sheep in need of the heavenly King's shepherding.

There are times in this life that cause us to feel desolate and alone, but we aren't either if we can say, "The Lord is *my* shepherd." The quiet, lonely moments have a purpose. He leads us to those times and makes us stop. God brings us to a green pasture, a place where he can feed us. He leads us "beside still waters" so that we are able to drink in what we need to survive and thrive.

We are sheep that need his care, and he knows when we need to stop. We need to rest and be fed while we are protected and cared for. There is a reason God will make your life come to a stop, to a fork in the road, to a time of indecision, or even a time of recognizing your *lostness*. God wants to restore your soul.

If you will acknowledge you are a sheep and allow the Lord to be your Shepherd, you will be led to exchange your plans for his. You might need to give up some things to gain what God wants you to have instead. You should not leave the pasture until your soul has been restored. Only then can he lead you "in paths of righteousness for his name's sake" (v. 3). A restored soul is essential for everyone in the Lord's flock because it is the only way to live right with God. He is the Good Shepherd, and he expertly knows how to care for his lambs.

Why can God's people walk through the valleys of our lives without fearing evil? Psalm 23:4 provides the answer: God is *with us*. The rod was a long stick used to encourage the sheep to keep moving and also used to ward off a predator. The staff was curved and used to bring a sheep or a lamb back to the path when it strayed. Sometimes the staff was used to rescue the one who was falling or entangled.

The rod and staff might seem painful at times, but it is also our protection. God's "comfort" belongs to the sheep of his flock who walk closely with their Shepherd. We don't fear evil because we *belong* to God. We can even face the "valley of the shadow of death" and not fear what it might bring. Every valley has a beginning and an end. God's sheep will ultimately come out of their valleys and step into a better place.

What does life look like after the quiet, even lonely, time of restoration? After a journey through the valley? David provides a picture that he himself lived. He wrote, "You prepare a table before me in the presence of my enemies; you anoint my head with oil; my cup overflows" (v. 5). There is life after the valley and it is an abundant life. Our shepherd grows us to be more than a sheep would ever have been.

Sheep don't sit at tables. Sheep are not *anointed*, esteemed, and set apart for a higher purpose. Sheep don't drink from cups on their own. God's sheep grow to become his children and become "more than conquerors through him who loved us" (Romans 8:37).

What does life look like on the other side of the valley? King David writes, "Surely goodness and mercy shall follow me all the days of my life, and I shall dwell in the house of the Lord forever" (v. 6).

God's children have a Good Shepherd. Whatever valley we face in this life has a beginning and an end. And the Shepherd is with us, caring for us and guiding us through each moment. One day, the valley will end and we will find ourselves welcomed into the house of the Lord, and we will joyfully meet our Good Shepherd face-to-face. Heaven is promised to those who can say, "The Lord is *my* shepherd."

Our life's journey is blessed when we allow the Good Shepherd to guide our path. There will be pastures and valleys, but there is also "goodness and mercy" every day of our lives. And one day, we will arrive at our eternal home.

Can you and will you repeat the words, "The Lord is my shepherd; I shall not want"? Meditate and pray over the twenty-third Psalm until King David's words of praise are yours as well. The Good Shepherd has a plan for your life, and you can be "more than a conqueror" when you follow his guidance and receive his good and merciful care. ◆

PRAYER

Thank you, Lord, for being my good shepherd. Your care, your rest, and your presence are what I most need. Keep me, Lord, in a quiet place until my soul is restored and I can once again walk your path before me. I ask you to guide me, protect me, and pull me back to you when I stray. Your presence surrounds me and your mercy and love sustain me—my heart is filled to overflowing. Help me walk in your will until, one day, I walk in your presence. Until that day, Amen

ADAPTED FROM PSALM 23

A GREAT CALM

SCRIPTURE

God's word as your Shepherd

"It is the Lord who goes before you. He will be with you; he will not leave you or forsake you. Do not fear or be dismayed."
DEUTERONOMY 31:8

"I will go before you and level the exalted places, I will break in pieces the doors of bronze and cut through the bars of iron, I will give you the treasures of darkness and the hoards in secret places, that you may know that it is I, the Lord, the God of Israel, who call you by your name."
ISAIAH 45:2–3

"The Lord was going before them in a pillar of cloud by day to lead them on the way, and in a pillar of fire by night to give them light, that they might travel by day and by night."
EXODUS 13:21

"The Lord will fight for you, and you have only to be silent."
EXODUS 14:14

"He will tend his flock like a shepherd; he will gather the lambs in his arms; he will carry them in his bosom, and gently lead those that are with young."
ISAIAH 40:11

"I am the good shepherd. The good shepherd lays down his life for the sheep."
JOHN 10:11

"I give them eternal life, and they will never perish, and no one will snatch them out of my hand."
JOHN 10:28

"The heavens declare
the glory of God,
and the sky above
proclaims his
handiwork."

PSALM 19:1

Creation reveals the greatness of God

When it seems like other things have become more powerful or influential in your life than God, where do you go or what do you do to *refocus* and regain a sense of peace? Jesus knew he had to withdraw from the noise and press of the crowds too. One of the most powerful revelations of God's nature *is nature* itself. If all we had was the natural world around us, we would still be able to know the greatness of God.

Paul wrote, "For his invisible attributes, namely, his eternal power and divine nature, have been clearly perceived, ever since the creation of the world, in the things that have been made" (Romans 1:20). God reveals his glory in each sunrise and sunset. God reveals his infinite nature in the oceans and the expanse of the stars. God reveals his compassionate love in the way a bird watches over her nest. God reveals hope and promise each time one season consistently transitions to the next.

No matter how hot the summer is, we know cooler days are coming. No matter how icy the winters become, we know the snow will thaw and the trees will bud again. Spring and fall speak of God's provision and care. He gives us time to prepare for the future.

God didn't have to create this planet as he did. He could have created us to survive in less beautiful and magnificent surroundings. He chose to create this world in a way that would reveal his nature, his "invisible attributes."

Could it be that the Lord created the seasons as his consistent yet ever-changing reminders of the passage of time? Did he want us to notice that time is continually moving us forward, to a destination we can't yet see? Last year is over and will never repeat again. Changes in nature are an earthly experience that stand in contrast to the unchanging nature of God. He created all things for his good purpose. He created the world like he did so that every human being would have no excuse for ignoring their Creator. Creation shouts *there is a God* and these are his "attributes."

- When you need to hope things will get better, look to the changing seasons. Our troubles will transition with time as well.
- When it seems as if God's presence is being removed from our culture, remember that all of creation is a revelation of his divine nature. God is ever-present in our world, and no one will have an excuse for not recognizing his powerful presence in each day.

- When it seems like the reality of God has grown too small in your own life, retreat to that place in nature where his reality is undeniable. Sit by an ocean. Walk in the mountains. Or just sit quietly in a park. God's creative genius is everywhere, if we pause with the intention of seeing him.

Scripture says, "Draw near to God, and He will draw near to you" (James 4:8). When you want a reminder of the greatness of God, search his creation. He reminds us we have great hope in all he has promised eternally, simply by glimpsing the world around us now. ◆

PRAYER

Father, you know all things. You have
power over all things and you are present
in all things. Your creation speaks to your
greatness, and I am in awe of who you
are. Lord, may I take time to stop rushing
through my life, hoping to meet self–
imposed deadlines. Instead, Lord, may
I rush to that quiet spot, to see the sun rise
and remember your divine greatness. Each
day is new and one day closer to eternity.
I live with hope for a life in heaven because
of all you have revealed of yourself on earth.

A GREAT CALM

SCRIPTURE

God's word explains the natural world and his creative nature

"For his invisible attributes, namely, his eternal power and divine nature, have been clearly perceived, ever since the creation of the world, in the things that have been made. So they are without excuse."
ROMANS 1:20

"All things were made through him, and without him was not any thing made that was made."
JOHN 1:3

"The heavens declare the glory of God, and the sky above proclaims his handiwork."
PSALM 19:1

"The heavens declare the glory of God, and the sky above proclaims his handiwork."
COLOSSIANS 1:16

"You are the Lord, you alone. You have made the heaven, the heaven of heavens, with all their host, the earth and all that is on it, the seas and all that is in them; and you preserve all of them; and the host of heaven worships you."
NEHEMIAH 9:6

"By faith we understand that the universe was created by the word of God, so that what is seen was not made out of things that are visible."
HEBREWS 11:3

"Have you not known? Have you not heard? The Lord is the everlasting God, the Creator of the ends of the earth. He does not faint or grow weary; his understanding is unsearchable."
ISAIAH 40:28

"Worthy are you, our Lord and God, to receive glory and honor and power, for you created all things, and by your will they existed and were created."
REVELATION 4:11

"The Lord is near to
the brokenhearted and
saves the crushed
in spirit."

PSALM 34:18

The time to get ready for that day is this day

My grandmother watched four of her sons go to war. Only three came home. My mom still remembers sitting beside her grieving mom on the log pile, after the soldiers with the yellow papers had left. She wanted to comfort her mom and couldn't. It was the first time she ever remembers seeing her mom cry.

A friend had a birthday meal waiting for her daughter's arrival, only to have the meal grow cold. While the family had gathered, her daughter had been attacked and killed by a crazed person. He used the money that he had stolen from her account to buy a pizza for himself and his dog right after he took the innocent girl's life.

Another friend went to dinner with her mom, only to return home and find her son had taken his life.

In the first few years of our ministry, we were serving our first church in Mansfield, Texas. My husband and I were expecting our first child, and I had been tired and sickly all day. We had just fallen asleep when the phone rang. A teenager in the church had drowned. The father was asking if we could come to his house and tell his wife when she returned home. I was twenty-six years old and had no experience for a moment like this. Even to this day, if I close my eyes, I remember the mom's agonized scream.

We all have watched people endure this level of grief and might even have known it personally. That kind of grief is among our greatest fears.

I have been a pastor's wife for almost forty years, and I'm still in ministry. I'm never ready for the next phone call. I never have words that are adequate. I know the eternal truth, but in those most difficult moments it sounds hollow and insufficient for the present pain.

I also have learned to live with the knowledge that the next phone call *will* come. It is the road God has chosen for each of our lives. And I consider it a holy privilege to walk through the worst moments of life with people I care about.

The lessons I learned at twenty-six are still the lessons I hold close today. We don't like to think about grief, but it is a very real part of life, and it is easier if you visit those thoughts before you have to live with them. If you want to be ready or, truthfully, as ready as possible:

- Realize the best time to get ready for the hard times is right now. It is much easier to take the punch if you have built up the spiritual muscle to handle its impact. Don't worry about facing grief; accept that at some point in this lifetime, you will live with it. Be strong in the Lord now and it will be easier to find strength in the Lord when you need it most.

- You will need Jesus to be your shield. The Lord will protect you with a barrier you will later describe as feeling numb. I like to think of it as the Lord taking the hits so you don't have to. He is our shield, and you can trust him to protect you from some of the pain. Your heart *will* get better, even though it will be forever changed.

- You will need Jesus to author your thoughts. People will flood you with words, hoping to make you feel better. Jesus will speak to you and filter their words so that he can guide you into truth. You will need to submit all of your thoughts to Christ because only some are worth keeping. As Paul taught, "Take every thought captive to obey Christ" (2 Corinthians 10:5). Ask God for the wisdom and discernment to know what he is saying so you can discard what only "feels like truth."

- You will need to resist the devil if you want him to flee from your thoughts so you can embrace the Lord's. Jesus knew the devil was real and worth fighting; we should too.

There is so much more, but this knowledge has been a great help to me in times of grief. Our choices now will impact our grief later. We should live in such a way that as we sit at a funeral or walk by a grieving person's side, we can do so with as few regrets as possible. Let's not wait to admire a person until their funeral or wait to express our appreciation, love, and friendship until after they are gone. We shouldn't hesitate to bring comfort now. We need to live in such a way that regrets don't have to be part of our grief.

If I were God, people wouldn't have to grieve. But I'm not perfect and God is. I don't know why God allows us to grieve. I do know that times of grief are one of the few times in life when people are forced to realize that their *only* help is God. Many of the people you have known will become *proven* friends during the difficult times. Times of grief teach us a great deal as we work through the tough days and allow God to redeem our pain.

Even after all these years, I remain *unaccustomed* to grief. I hope I always will be. I want to help people realize that grief is as important to our lives as our hope and joy. Everything in this life has an eternal significance—even our grief.

It seems funny. We always expect our joys to be momentary but don't usually feel that way about grief. We should expect to experience every earthly emotion common to man. Have you strengthened your faith for the phone call that will surely come someday?

I do know one thing that will ease the pain of grief more quickly. Will you grieve with comfort, knowing the person you grieve has received a home in heaven? If not, that should be your most important concern for them today. We will grieve differently if we can grieve with hope.

Make choices right now that will have you sitting at the funeral thinking, "Thank you, Lord. I have no regrets." ◆

PRAYER

Lord, when the tears come, help me remember you cried tears of grief as well. But for today, Lord, tell me who to call, who to text, and how I should care. May I be your hands and feet in this world and help people walk toward you, as we walk toward eternity. May there be few regrets, and may we have great hope as we live, and as we grieve, for your glory.

A GREAT CALM

SCRIPTURE

God's word gives hope for our grief

"I have said these things to you, that in me you may have peace. In the world you will have tribulation. But take heart; I have overcome the world."
JOHN 16:33

"The Lord is near to the brokenhearted and saves the crushed in spirit."
PSALM 34:18

"For I consider that the sufferings of this present time are not worth comparing with the glory that is to be revealed to us."
ROMANS 8:18

"He heals the brokenhearted and binds up their wounds."
PSALM 147:3

"But we do not want you to be uninformed, brother, about those who are asleep, that you may not grieve as others do who have no hope."
1 THESSALONIANS 4:13

"Jesus said to her, 'I am the resurrection and the life. Whoever believes in me, though he die, yet shall he live."
JOHN 11:25

A GREAT CALM

"Casting all your anxieties on him, because he cares for you."
1 PETER 5:7

"He will wipe away every tear from their eyes, and death shall be no more, neither shall there be mourning, nor crying, nor pain anymore, for the former things have passed away."
REVELATION 21:4

"And the peace of God, which surpasses all understanding, will guard your hearts and your minds in Christ Jesus."

PHILIPPIANS 4:7

When the tears are ours, his peace is promised

How do we know Jesus understands our trials? My favorite answers to that question come from the book of John. John was the "beloved disciple." Some might say that the Apostle John was the best friend Christ had in his earthly ministry. Jesus loved John as a brother and knew he was trustworthy. From the cross, the Lord asked John to take care of Mary, his mother.

John 13–20 are some of the most heart-wrenching words in Scripture, written by John, with a heart that understood loss. John was writing down all that Jesus had said when he knew his death was imminent. Jesus wanted to prepare his disciples for all that lay ahead. In John 14, Jesus tells his disciples that God will send them the Helper, the Holy Spirit, and he will be their teacher. The Spirit will help them to remember *everything* Jesus taught.

Then Jesus said something remarkable to them. He was looking at a group of men he had chosen as his inner circle. He was looking at his closest friends on earth and one who would become his betrayer. He told them they didn't need to be troubled or afraid (John 14:27).

Was he looking at John's face, the face of his best friend, when he said *you don't need to be troubled or afraid?* At the very least, we know John was watching him. It is his gospel that most completely records these moments. It's comforting to lean on Jesus' words to his disciples when he told them not to fear the coming days.

The reason the disciples didn't need to feel troubled or afraid is because of the Helper—the Holy Spirit. John 14:27 is one of my favorite descriptions of the Holy Spirit who indwells every believer. Jesus said, "Peace I leave with you; my peace I give to you. Not as the world gives do I give to you." *Then* Jesus said, "Let not your hearts be troubled, neither let them be afraid."

Jesus said his peace would be different from the peace the world could give. When Jesus promised to give his peace, he was promising his actual Presence through the Holy Spirit.

When we go through a tough time, people will surround us with kind thoughts and words. But, Jesus will *fill us* with the same peace that carried him to Calvary and the same peace that enabled most of those men in that room to preach the gospel to a hostile world. Jesus said his peace isn't the peace the world can give.

The key to facing pain in this world is to understand that the peace you need most is the peace Jesus promised to give.

- Receive people's well-intentioned words, but lean on those who pray for you.
- Be grateful for the help people offer, but pursue the help that only Jesus can give.
- It is natural to become angry or disappointed with God for allowing the tough times. His peace, however, is available when we remember God always has a plan to redeem the tough times for his good purpose.
- Remember, the people in heaven are not missing anything. Ask Jesus for the peace you need as you miss them each day, but trust and believe that heaven is truly paradise.

When Jesus knew he would soon die, he promised John and the others he would still be with them. The Holy Spirit is the continued earthly ministry of Christ. He is the comfort and compassion of Christ. His peace is unique, and it is the promise of Christ. Pursue *that peace*, and you will find it—even in the tough times of life. ◆

PRAYER

Lord, I need your peace, the peace of your Holy Spirit, your presence. Thank you for those who have cared and provided me with your comfort through their prayers. Jesus, you understand. Only your peace can calm our souls and quiet our minds. But it is also your peace that moves us forward. One day we will live in paradise. Until then, help us to live joyfully with that hope.

A GREAT CALM

SCRIPTURE

God's word about the peace of God's Holy Spirit

"May the God of hope fill you with all joy and peace in believing, so that by the power of the Holy Spirit you may abound in hope."
ROMANS 15:13

"And the peace of God, which surpasses all understanding, will guard your hearts and your minds in Christ Jesus."
PHILIPPIANS 4:7

"Peace I leave with you; my peace I give to you. Not as the world gives do I give to you. Let not your hearts be troubled, neither let them be afraid."
JOHN 14:27

"You, however, are not in the flesh but in the Spirit, if in fact the Spirit of God dwells in you. Anyone who does not have the Spirit of Christ does not belong to him."
ROMANS 8:9

"And let the peace of Christ rule in your hearts, to which indeed you were called in one body. And be thankful."
COLOSSIANS 3:15

A GREAT CALM

"You keep him in perfect peace whose mind is stayed on you, because he trusts in you."
ISAIAH 26:3

"But the fruit of the Spirit is love, joy, peace, patience, kindness, goodness, faithfulness, gentleness, self-control; against such things there is no law."
GALATIANS 5:22-23

"Therefore, since we have been justified by faith, we have peace with God through our Lord Jesus Christ."
ROMANS 5:1

"My flesh and my heart may fail, but God is the strength of my heart and my portion forever."

PSALM 73:26

You can live well, even in grief

Have you ever watched people on one of those moving sidewalks in the airports? Some stand still and let the belt carry them along. Others walk on the belt so they can reach their destination a little faster. Some people stand alone, and others are surrounded by family or friends. It is a picture of sorts, of the different ways people move through their earthly lives.

Some people embrace change and the speed of life; others don't. Some people find it easier to face forward; others want to turn around and see where they have come from. But everyone is moving forward, regardless of which way they are facing.

When we or someone we care about must move on with life after a tough time, it's important to remember that God wants us to live well—in all seasons of life. Everyone accepts change differently, and only God knows how long a chapter of life should last. If someone loses a spouse, especially after years and years of marriage, the two have become one. What does life look like when half of it no longer exists? Sometimes the new normal can't feel normal. That could be a time to just step on that moving conveyor, face forward, and allow God to carry you. If it takes more time to arrive at the next place, that is fine. You are still moving forward.

A fundamental truth of Scripture can help define times of change and infuse life with hope for the future. Romans 8:28 teaches us that God intends to "work all things together for good" if we love God and allow our lives to move forward for his good purpose. If you are alive, God wants you to live well. Living well is living the individual plan God has worked out for your life.

It takes time for God to work in us and to work his plan for our good. We shouldn't hurry those who are struggling simply because we miss their joy and want them to feel better. That is trying to work things for our good, not God's. Grief can honor the person who was loved. Change can bring about a new perspective or purpose for life.

Grieving people should be allowed to cry. Tired people should be allowed to rest. Confused people should be allowed to think. If God created us with tears and with the ability to process thoughts, he must have intended for us to do those things. I often describe our tears as God's way of emptying the grief from our hearts and lives. Quiet time alone is often our chance to experience God's presence and receive his good plans. As grief abates, the tears fall less often. As we are led to conclusions, our confusion fades and our choices become clearer.

How do we live well when we have to live without a person we love? We live our days with heavenly priorities. How do we move forward even when the future is confusing, even frightening? The Apostle Paul understood that challenge.

Paul had endured many things in his life. He was quite possibly alienated from his family when he left the Jewish faith to become a Christian. We know Paul had to live with the grief he had caused others because he had persecuted Christians as heretics. He also knew his actions would have led some of his Jewish brothers and sisters to turn from Christ as their Messiah. After his experience on the road to Damascus, he understood and grieved what he had done. Throughout his ministry, Paul lost friends, suffered failures, and faced an unknown future. Later, Paul wrote to the church in Rome, saying, "I consider that the sufferings of this present time are not worth comparing with the glory that is to be revealed to us" (Romans 8:18).

Paul had moved through his grief and was so focused on his ministry that he had come to view his hardships on earth with an eternal perspective. People had died because of Paul's abuse, but he found comfort knowing they were fully alive and well in heaven.

Never doubt the security we have in Christ. He has a plan to bless and use each day we dedicate to him. When you grieve, pray for an eternal perspective to bring you peace. Joy will come whenever the morning comes. Some grief seems like a long, long night. Take your time, cry your tears, and hold fast to the life God has given you. He has a plan for your life in the days ahead.

Paul apparently spent three years in exile, processing his experience on the road to Damascus, before he began his new ministry as a Christian. Nearly everything in his life had changed. But, Paul eventually was spiritually prepared to move ahead with God's Spirit knowing that "for those who love God all things work together for good" (Romans 8:28).

If you are in a similar place, Jesus wants you to live well with his blessings. It may take you many years to feel blessed. You may be the person who is simply standing on that moving sidewalk, and that is all right. God is still moving you forward, and you will reach your destination—in due time. ◆

PRAYER

Father, may I remember the purpose of life doesn't change just because the plan does. When I grieve, may I know it is only for a season. When I simply need to be still, help me to peacefully step aside from those who want to move faster. Keep moving me forward so I can reach that time I am living more fully with you. May each day be one step closer to hearing you say, "Well done, my good and faithful servant." For that goal, and for your glory, I will continue to live well as you work all things, even the hard times, for your good purpose.

A GREAT CALM

SCRIPTURE

God's word for our grief

"For I know the plans I have for you, declares the Lord, plans for welfare and not for evil, to give you a future and a hope."
JEREMIAH 29:11

"I know that you can do all things, and that no purpose of yours can be thwarted."
JOB 42:2

"Therefore, my beloved, as you have always obeyed, so now, not only as in my presence but much more in my absence, work out your own salvation with fear and trembling, for it is God who works in you, both to will and to work for his good pleasure."
PHILIPPIANS 2:12–13

"My flesh and my heart may fail, but God is the strength of my heart and my portion forever."
PSALM 73:26

"The Lord is my rock and my fortress and my deliverer, my God, my rock, in whom I take refuge, my shield, and the horn of my salvation, my stronghold."
PSALM 18:2

"So also you have sorrow now, but I will see you again, and your hearts will rejoice, and no one will take your joy from you."
JOHN 16:22

"Jesus said to her, 'I am the resurrection and the life. Whoever believes in me, though he die, yet shall he live, and everyone who lives and believes in me shall never die. Do you believe this?'"
JOHN 11:25-26

"I have said these things to you, that in me you may have peace. In the world you will have tribulation. But take heart; I have overcome the world."
JOHN 16:33

"I cry out to God Most High, to God who will fulfill his purpose for me."

PSALM 57:2

Count it all joy

There are some verses that seem more difficult to obey than others. When Peter fled from Jerusalem after being imprisoned, it is believed that James, the Lord's brother, became the leader of the Christian church in that ancient city.

James' epistle to the early church created a heated debate among the people who were deciding which books should belong in our canon, the Bible. Several felt James' letter did not belong and that James was not a true *apostle*. Theologians have continued the debate through the years. Martin Luther called the book of James a "straw-epistle" and, in his opinion, it did not have "doctrinal value."

James is one of the most practical books in all the New Testament. Christians are blessed by the letter, which is rich with encouragement and practical advice about how to live our Christian faith and witness.

How interesting that James began his letter by saying, "Count it all joy, my brothers, when you meet trials of various kinds" (James 1:2). The key to joy might just be found in the simple use of the word *all*.

James said we can count *everything* in our lives as joy, trials included, because it is when our faith is "tested" that it produces "steadfastness" in our lives (James 1:3). When can trials bring us joy? When those trials strengthen our faith.

I've heard so many Christians who have come through a rough time say something like, "I don't ever want to go through that again, but I am blessed because of all I learned from it." They are able to count it as joy. As the book of James describes, their steadfastness has had "its full effect," and they have come through it having been "perfected" through the tough times (James 1:4).

When we need joy, we should view the events of our lives, even the trials, as opportunities. If God has allowed something to impact your life, he already knows how it could "perfect" your faith. Oftentimes, the most direct road to joy is discovered by recognizing God's hand as he works to redeem the tough times for our good.

How is it possible to count it *all* joy? James 1:5 is a first step: "If any of you lacks wisdom, let him ask God, who gives generously to all without reproach, and it will be given to him." When we need God's joy, we should ask him for the wisdom to discern the ways he is redeeming even the trials of our lives, to perfect our faith.

Joy isn't about what *happens* in our lives; that is happiness. Joy is about how God is at work in the things that happen for his greater kingdom purpose. Joy is about our eternal good. God can and will redeem *anything* he allows in our lives.

When the trials come, we can know God loves us and is already at work with his redemptive purpose. We can "count it all joy." ◆

PRAYER

Thank you, Father, that you use all things in our lives to be a source of perfected joy. We praise you, even for the trials, because of how you will redeem them for our eternal good. Help us to remain steadfast in our faith so that your redemption will have its full effect. We know, God, that is our joy.

A GREAT CALM

SCRIPTURE

God's word about his work in our lives

> "For we are his workmanship, created in Christ Jesus for good works, which God prepared beforehand, that we should walk in them."
> **EPHESIANS 2:10**

> "I know that you can do all things, and that no purpose of yours can be thwarted."
> **JOB 42:2**

> "So, whether you eat or drink, or whatever you do, do all to the glory of God."
> **1 CORINTHIANS 10:31**

> "The Lord of hosts has sworn: 'As I have planned, so shall it be, and as I have purposed, so shall it stand.'"
> **ISAIAH 14:24**

> "I cry out to God Most High, to God who will fulfill his purpose for me."
> **PSALM 57:2**

"And the world is passing away along with its desires, but whoever does the will of God abides forever."

1 JOHN 2:17

"I glorified you on earth, having accomplished the work that you gave me to do."

JOHN 17:4

"For everyone who has been born of God overcomes the world. And this is the victory that has overcome the world—our faith."

1 JOHN 5:4

"If we confess our sins, he is faithful and just to forgive us our sins and to cleanse us from all unrighteousness."

1 JOHN 1:9

All of us need a clean heart

We all know someone who was hurt by a church or one of God's people. Some say they will never go back to church again. Every Christian hurts others, often unknowingly. We all say things we wish we hadn't said. All of us have rushed past an opportunity to help. We can hurt people and hurt their souls. We are human beings, and we have all "fallen short of God's glory" (Romans 3:23). Whether we have been wronged or we have done wrong, those are the times we need a clean heart.

Scripture says that King David was called a man after God's own heart (1 Samuel 13:14), but, years later, he chose to sin with

Bathsheba. If King David could allow himself to sin, we should expect to have weaknesses and failures ourselves. Everyone sins, but it is usually true that everyone also commits a grievous sin at some point in our lives. It's not that God *ranks* our sin, but some sins have greater consequences to us and others.

We all end up in a wrong place, at a wrong time, and make a wrong choice. King David was supposed to be with his men on the battlefield. Instead, he was in his palace, lusting after the wife of one of his faithful soldiers. In 2 Samuel 11, the whole, ugly story unfolds.

Most of us can look back to a low point in our walk with the Lord too. After I had walked through a dark time in my own life, I finally was able to sit with David's Psalm 51. I needed a clean heart. I wanted a clean heart and life. I have continued to go back to Psalm 51 since that time. David wrote this psalm after his sin with Bathsheba because he needed a clean heart. It is one of the best *spiritual cleanups* I have found in Scripture.

These words are not just for the times we have done wrong; it is also a good word for the times we have been wronged. In either circumstance, David's words help.

Read through the psalm as a prayer for your own life. If necessary, read it over and over until David's heart and song become yours. But, if you have suffered because of someone else's sins, you can read Psalm 51 as your prayer for that person's life. We need to pray for our *enemies*, and this passage of Scripture is a good help when our own thoughts and words fail.

David pleads with God for mercy. There is something incredibly profound about picturing an earthly king submitting his heart and life to the heavenly King. David understood that even his position of power and authority was nothing without God's blessings. In abject humility, he sought the Lord.

Sometimes people with power over our lives abuse that power. Sometimes we make that choice ourselves. The road to a clean heart begins on our knees, admitting that no one can be right unless they are first right with God. When we sin, our first need is to realize we sinned against God as well.

- We hurt God when our witness is corrupted.
- We hurt God when our sin separates our life from his blessings.
- We hurt God when we hurt others.
- We hurt God when we don't forgive ourselves and others.

The goal when our lives have been damaged by sin is the same goal King David had when he wrote this psalm from his broken heart. David said, "Create in me a clean heart, O God, and renew a right spirit within me. Cast me not away from your presence, and take not your Holy Spirit from me. Restore to me the joy of your salvation, and uphold me with a willing spirit" (Psalm 51:10–12).

In the Old Testament, the Holy Spirit's indwelling was not constant. The New Covenant through Christ changed that. A Christian never needs to ask God not to take his Holy Spirit from our lives. We *do need* to ask him to forgive us from "quenching the Holy Spirit" by our sinful choices.

- We need to stop separating our lives from God's blessings because of continued sin.
- We need a right spirit, a right relationship with God.

- We need the joy that comes from knowing we are saved eternally.
- We need a willing spirit that walks submitted to the will of God's Spirit and leadership.

If you knew you would enter glory soon, what would you wish you had *fixed* before arriving in heaven? That's not a rhetorical question; that is a question each of us should continually ask and answer until heaven becomes our home.

One of my favorite messages in Psalm 51 is verse 13. David wanted his relationship restored so that he could help others know his God and learn from his lessons.

When you honestly plead with God for a clean heart, he will give it. One of the first people you need to forgive is yourself. God wants you to live a life that reflects his love, his mercy, and his blessings to others. And if you need to forgive someone who has hurt you, understand that the *only forgiveness* you should give is the forgiveness you have received. Human forgiveness won't produce a clean heart—God's forgiveness will.

David wrote, "The sacrifices of God are a broken spirit; a broken and contrite heart, O God, you will not despise" (Psalm 51:17).

If your heart is broken because of your sin, or someone else's, God has the power to mend it. Allow King David to *teach* you God's ways (Psalm 51:13). David's sin with Bathsheba was terrible, and a good man and an innocent baby died. If God redeemed and restored David, he can do the same for you.

What did David's redemption look like? David and Bathsheba named him Solomon, their son, who became the next king of

Israel. Whatever sin has caused you to grieve, ask God for a clean heart. Redemption, for ourselves and others, is our high and worthy goal.

I pray you will have David's heart as you read David's words. Read, pray and live with Psalm 51 until David's prayer has truly become yours. You deserve a clean heart too. ◆

PRAYER

Oh God, because of your unfailing love and abundant mercy, I ask you to have compassion on me! By your divine grace, cleanse me from my sins. I know I have been disobedient in your sight, and my heart is broken because I have grieved you. I have sinned against you and your judgment against me is perfect and justified.
I was born into sin, Lord, and only you can forgive me and teach me your ways of righteousness. Only by your divine grace am I made clean.
By the blood of Jesus, you make me whiter than snow. Let me experience joy and gladness again. My soul is crushed by the weight of my sin yet I rejoice in your transforming grace. Cleanse me so completely that the stain of my sin no longer exists. Create in me a clean heart, O God, and renew a right spirit within me, so that I may

experience your presence and hear the voice of your Holy Spirit within me. Restore the joy of my salvation and champion me with a heart that is willing to follow you. Then I will bear witness to your great name and others will see you in me. Because you have showered me with your mercy and grace, I will proclaim your righteousness and sing your praise. If all you wanted was my sacrifice, I would give it, but a sincere heart is what you desire from me and for me. My broken spirit and repentant heart are the offerings that bring you pleasure. These are the offerings I give you now, in the merciful name of Jesus, Amen.

ADAPTED FROM PSALM 51

A GREAT CALM

SCRIPTURE

God's word about forgiveness

> "If we confess our sins, he is faithful and just to forgive us our sins and to cleanse us from all unrighteousness."
> **1 JOHN 1:9**

> "Bearing with one another and, if one has a complaint against another, forgiving each other; as the Lord has forgiven you, so you also must forgive."
> **COLOSSIANS 3:13**

> "And forgive us our debts, as we also have forgiven our debtors."
> **MATTHEW 6:12**

> "No temptation has overtaken you that is not common to man. God is faithful, and he will not let you be tempted beyond your ability, but with the temptation he will also provide the way of escape, that you may be able to endure it."
> **1 CORINTHIANS 10:13**

> "Whoever covers an offense seeks love, but he who repeats a matter separates close friends."
> **PROVERBS 17:9**

"Be kind to one another, tenderhearted, forgiving one another, as God in Christ forgave you."
EPHESIANS 4:32

"And whenever you stand praying, forgive, if you have anything against anyone, so that your Father also who is in heaven may forgive you your trespasses."
MARK 11:25

"Therefore, confess your sins to one another and pray for one another, that you may be healed. The prayer of a righteous person has great power as it is working."
JAMES 5:16

"Let the wicked forsake his way, and the unrighteous man his thoughts; let him return to the Lord, that he may have compassion on him, and to our God, for he will abundantly pardon."
ISAIAH 55:7

"Come now, let us reason together, says the Lord: though your sins are like scarlet, they shall be as white as snow; though they are red like crimson, they shall become like wool."
ISAIAH 1:18

"If then you have been raised with Christ, seek the things that are above, where Christ is, seated at the right hand of God."

COLOSSIANS 3:1

Enter faith with eyes wide open

My dad used to say that the only people who wanted to own a swimming pool were the people who had never owned a swimming pool. I have to smile at his wisdom. A swimming pool is a LOT of work. The water needs to be checked on a regular basis so that the chemicals stay in balance. The pool often needs to be cleaned because debris is floating on the surface. The equipment seems to break quite often and needs repairs. The maintenance can be tedious, especially during the winter months when we aren't able to swim. But on those hot days when you enjoy the chance to cool off and relax in the pool, the maintenance seems completely worth it.

Caring for a swimming pool is a pretty good comparison to caring for our souls. It is constant and costly work too. If you want to own a pool, go into it with eyes wide open. It is going to require a LOT of costly maintenance. We should step into our faith decision with that same attitude.

People become disillusioned sometimes after realizing their decision to make Christ their Lord came at a price. That is increasingly true in our culture today. A public, strong witness can cost a person their job. Sometimes choosing to be godly can cost a person some friendships. A faithful walk with Christ certainly costs us the right to be self-absorbed, the right to make certain business deals, the right to say and do certain things, and the chance to feel right about what is wrong. Not to mention, an obedient walk with God costs us a percentage of all that we earn.

Sometimes it seems like the Bible has promised us joy, peace, and blessing, but our spiritual life feels broken, dull, or just less than we thought it would be. The spiritual solution for those kinds of thoughts is provided in the promise Jesus made to his disciples in the Upper Room. Jesus was preparing them for his death when he *promised* them, "In the world you will have tribulation. But take heart; I have overcome the world" (John 16:33).

The Bible promises joy but also sadness. The Bible promises peace but also problems. If we really want God's word to be our strength, we need to consider all the promises in the Bible. A lot of our weariness with God, or even our disillusionment, comes from misunderstanding God's promises for our earthly lives. As you consider *all* of God's words, remember:

- Psalms are not words of promise but words of praise for what God is *able* to do.
- Most of God's promises are permanently true for our eternal lives, not our earthly lives.
- God's promises are often based on his ability to bless our choices. God *can't bless* choices he cannot endorse.

- God's plan is to redeem our mistakes for his great good, but we must love him and be called to his good purpose (Romans 8:28).

There has probably never been a pool salesman who emphasized how costly it would be to *maintain* a pool after it is built. Very few people build a pool knowing all that lies ahead. We tend to witness to our faith in much the same style. For the sake of our witness and for the sake of others, we need to know *all* that God has promised from the pages of his word. Our spiritual lives will require a lot of maintenance too.

In this world, there will be hard times for everyone, Christians included. The good news is that we, like Jesus, will one day *overcome* this world and enter perfection. Don't grow weary because your faith seems like hard work or comes with challenges. One day, it will be completely worth it! Christians will step into heaven and find that every moment is good and every promise is permanent.

Until then, "taste and see" that the Lord is good! ◆

PRAYER

Father, help me remember that you never promised life on earth would be like life eternal. May I lower my expectations for this life and live instead for my eternal life. May I share my faith with others with honesty and biblical expectations. This world will have "tribulations," but thank you for ensuring we would overcome—and one day live joyfully with you, forever.

SCRIPTURE

God's word for the work of sanctification

"Sanctify them in the truth; your word is truth."
JOHN 17:17

"I have been crucified with Christ. It is no longer I who live, but Christ who lives in me. And the life I now live in the flesh I live by faith in the Son of God, who loved me and gave himself for me."
GALATIANS 2:20

"If then you have been raised with Christ, seek the things that are above, where Christ is, seated at the right hand of God."
COLOSSIANS 3:1

"But grow in the grace and knowledge of our Lord and Savior Jesus Christ. To him be the glory both now and to the day of eternity."
2 PETER 3:18

"But you are a chosen race, a royal priesthood, a holy nation, a people for his own possession, that you may proclaim the excellencies of him who called you out of darkness into his marvelous light."
1 PETER 2:9

"Whatever you do, work heartily, as for the Lord and not for men, knowing that from the Lord you will receive the inheritance as your reward. You are serving the Lord Christ."
COLOSSIANS 3:23-24

"For in this way there will be richly provided for you an entrance into the eternal kingdom of our Lord and Savior Jesus Christ."
2 PETER 1:11

"Behold! I tell you a mystery. We shall not all sleep, but we shall all be changed, in a moment, in the twinkling of an eye, at the last trumpet. For the trumpet will sound, and the dead will be raised imperishable, and we shall be changed."
1 CORINTHIANS 15:51-52

AFTERWORD

Daily pursue the great calm of Christ

Jesus taught his followers to pray, "Give us this day our daily bread" (Matthew 6:11). One of the great truths of knowing and living God's word is that it must be consistently consumed. Life is a series of choices and changes. God is present with every Christian for each moment of his/her life because of his Holy Spirit. But it is a daily, moment-to-moment choice to welcome and embrace the Lord's presence and will.

Consider the great calm that descended upon the waters and eventually upon the disciples after Jesus had spoken his power over the winds and the sea. The disciples had been terrified, expecting their boat to be capsized by the crashing waves. Instead, they realized they were safe because of their teacher, whom they were coming to know and accept as their Messiah. Soon the disciples came to understand that being with Jesus didn't mean the great calm was permanent.

Jesus and his disciples landed early the next day on the opposite shore of the Sea of Galilee, in the region known as Gadarenes (Matthew 8:28). Scripture says, "Two demon-possessed men met him, coming out of the tombs, so fierce that no one could pass that way. And behold, they cried out, 'What have you to do with us, O Son of God? Have you come here to torment us before the time?'" (Matthew 8:28–29).

The disciples stepped out of their boat and walked straight into a different kind of storm. But, they walked this moment with Jesus as well. The disciples listened as Jesus spoke to the demons that controlled these men. Soon after, they watched as the demons "came out and went into the pigs, and behold the whole herd rushed down the steep bank into the sea and drowned in the waters" (Matthew 8:32).

In a short period of time, the disciples had heard Jesus preach his Sermon on the Mount to the large crowds that had gathered. Shortly after, they survived an intense storm and experienced the great calm Jesus spoke over them and the storm. Hours later, they experienced the exorcism of the demonic forces that controlled two dangerous men.

We often study those stories separately, not realizing they all occurred within a short period of time. And God planned it that way.

Our spiritual lives are strengthened moment to moment in every circumstance we yield to the presence of Christ. Our great calm is his gift to us in the stormy thoughts of the night, but it is also for the moments we face each day. We shouldn't ask God for his daily bread unless we intend to consume it. Manna wasn't good for very long. By the next day, it was too late to eat because it had spoiled.

Our great calm is his gift to us in the stormy thoughts of the night, but it is also for the moments we face each day.

I never fully understood what Paul meant when he said "pray without ceasing" (1 Thessalonians 5:17). I used to think only a monk could obey that verse. But, I misunderstood what Paul was teaching. The Holy Spirit is present, at work in our lives, all the time. There is never a moment of our lives that he is not with us, guiding our thoughts, our steps, and our Christian service—when we ask and if we listen. That is what it means to "pray without ceasing."

Every moment is a choice to recognize and be filled with God's

Holy Spirit and continue the earthly ministry of Christ as his Spirit guides our steps. Jesus wants to provide his great calm to every moment you face, but we have to choose to bring our calm from the boat to the shore. When we do, our lives become our witness to others of the power of Christ within us.

Scripture tells us the herdsmen who had been watching Jesus as he spoke to the demon-possessed men "fled" (Matthew 8:33). When the herdsmen went "into the city they told everything, especially what had happened to the demon-possessed men. And behold, all the city came out to meet Jesus" (Matthew 8:33–34). The power of Christ is interesting to those around us but not always accepted.

Christ in us is our strength and our witness. We can't be filled with the calm of Christ if we only judge our witness by the reactions of others. The rest of the story says the people "came out to meet Jesus, and when they saw him, they begged him to leave their region" (Matthew 8:34). They saw the power of Christ yet didn't want him.

If we want to maintain a great calm in our ever-changing situations, we will need to find our peace-filled assurance in Christ rather than the approval of the world. It has always been true that some are drawn to Christ and others run away.

We will need to find our peace-filled assurance in Christ...

Imagine how the disciples felt after witnessing the Sermon on the Mount, the storm Jesus calmed, and the demons that were cast into the pigs. They had fully experienced the divinity of Christ. These men walked daily in his presence for the next two years. But, remember these same men also ran from the Garden of Gethsemane and even denied knowing Jesus.

Ultimately, the great calm of Christ continually includes our dependence upon his great grace. We will always be imperfect until we are perfected one day in heaven. Christ understands, and so would each of his disciples.

Keep this book in a handy spot because life will bring you back to its pages. The storms will continue to rage until we dwell eternally in the continual light and presence of Christ. The best time to get ready for the hard times is today.

I pray that you live with the certainty that you are loved with a perfect love, even during the times it doesn't feel that way. God's word will strengthen your soul. God's purpose will provide your perspective. Every day, God's presence should be pursued as your highest priority. King David wrote, "So teach us to number our days so we may get a heart of wisdom" (Psalm 90:12).

I pray that you will continuously pursue the great calm of Christ as you walk daily in his Spirit.

REFLECTIONS

Jesus said, "The Helper, the Holy Spirit, whom the Father will send in my name, he will teach you all things and bring to your remembrance all that I have said to you" *(John 14:26)*.

Father God, I want to remember...

ABOUT FOUNDATIONS WITH JANET DENISON

FOUNDATIONS WITH JANET DENISON exists to teach people about the transforming power of Scripture through digital Bible study. We are dedicated to helping people learn how to study the Bible and apply God's truth to their lives. Please visit foundationswithjanet.org for more information about our available resources.

ABOUT DENISON MINISTRIES

DENISON MINISTRIES is a Christian nonprofit that seeks to transform the culture through Christ-centered content. The ministry accomplishes that through four distinct brands:

- **Denison Forum** (denisonforum.org) offers a biblical and redemptive perspective on current events through *The Daily Article* email newsletter and podcast, *The Denison Forum Podcast*, and many books and online resources.
- **Christian Parenting** (christianparenting.org) provides practical and spiritual resources, including an expansive podcast network, to help parents raise children to know and love the Lord.
- **First15** (first15.org) leads Christians into a transformative personal encounter with God through devotional readings, worship videos, and guided prayers.
- **Foundations** (foundationswithjanet.org) offers Bible study resources with blogs, videos, and biblical content for individual and small-group use.

Learn more at DenisonMinistries.org.

NOTES

"If you wake up": Eric J. Olson, Mayo Clinic, "Insomnia: How do I stay asleep?," August 23, 2019, https://www.mayoclinic.org/diseases-conditions/insomnia/expert-answers/insomnia/faq-20057824.

"Sometimes God calms the storm, but sometimes God lets the storm rage and calms his child." Leslie Gould, *The Amish Nanny* (Harvest House Publishers, 2011)